Knock Knock!

Jimmy Giggles

"I always laugh at myself. It makes life more fun."

— Jimmy Giggles

CONTENTS

Benefits of Jokes

Comedy, humor, and joke-telling have many positive benefits associated with it. Jokes can bring a smile to the face of others and put you in a great mood! Here are a few more benefits associated with joke-telling:

- Help you bond with friends and family
- Lighten tense situations
- Help you make friends
- Great conversation starters
- Perfect for texts and status updates

Share a joke with a friend today!

Funny Knock Knock Jokes

Knock knock!

Who's there?

Adam!

Adam who?

Adam up and tell me the total!

Knock knock!

Who's there?

Adelia!

Adelia who?

Adelia the cards after you cut the deck!

Knock knock!

Who's there?

Adeline!

Adeline who?

Adeline extra to the letter!

Knock knock!

Who's there?

Adolf!

Adolf who?

Adolf ball hit me in the mouth!

Knock knock!

Who's there?

Burglar!

Burglar who?

Burglars don't knock!

Knock knock!

Who's there?

Abbey!

Abbey who?

Abbey stung me on the nose!

Knock knock!

Who's there?

Aaron!

Aaron who?

Aaron the barber's floor!

Knock knock!

Who's there?

Underwear!

Underwear who?

Underwear my baby is tonight?

Knock knock!

Who's there?

Chuck!

Chuck who?

Chuck in a sandwich for lunch!

Knock knock!

Who's there?

Acid!

Acid who?

Accidently on purpose!

Knock knock!

Who's there?

Comic!

Comic who?

Comic and see me sometime!

Knock knock!

Who's there?

Cologne!

Cologne who?

Cologne me names won't help!

Knock knock!

Who's there?

Acis!

Acis who?

Acis spades!

Knock knock!

Who's there?

Ada!

Ada who?

A diamond is forever!

Knock knock!

Who's there?

Adair!

Adair who?

Adair once but now I'm bald now!

Knock knock!

Who's there?

Bacon!

Bacon who?

Bacon a cake for your birthday!

Knock knock!

Who's there?

Cindy!

Cindy who?

Cindy next one in please!

Knock knock!

Who's there?

Bach!

Bach who?

Bach to work!

Knock knock!

Who's there?

Curry!

Curry who?

Curry me back home will you!?

Knock knock!

Who's there?

Curly!

Curly who?

Curly Q!

Knock knock!

Who's there?

C's!

C's who?

C's the day!

Knock knock!

Who's there?

Crock and dial!

Crock and dial who?

Crock and dial Dundee!

Knock knock!

Who's there?

Adore!

Adore who?

Adore stands between us, open up!

Knock knock!

Who's there?

Banana!

Banana who?

Banana split so ice creamed!

Knock knock!

Who's there?

Closure!

Closure who?

Closure mouth when you eat!

Knock knock!

Who's there?

Cook!

Cook who?

Cuckoo yourself, I don't come here to be insulted!

Knock knock!

Who's there?

Cookie!

Cookie who?

Cookie quit and now I have to make all the food!

Knock knock!

Who's there?

Cole!

Cole who?

Cole as a cucumber!

Knock knock!

Who's there?

Cows!

Cows who?

Cows go moo not who!

Knock knock!

Who's there?

Cotton!

Cotton who?

Cotton a trap!

Knock knock!

Who's there?

Cod!

Cod who?

Cod red-handed!

Knock knock!

Who's there?

Clark!

Clark who?

Clark your car in the garage!

Knock knock!

Who's there?

Claude!

Claude who?

Claude up by the cat!

Knock knock!

Who's there?

Baby owl!

Baby owl who?

Baby owl see you later!

Knock knock!

Who's there?

Crete!

Crete who?

Crete to see you again!

Knock knock!

Who's there?

Albee!

Albee who?

Albee a monkey's uncle!

Knock knock!

Who's there?

Ahmed!

Ahmed who?

Ahmed a big mistake coming here!

Knock knock!

Who's there?

Boo!

Boo who?

Don't cry. It's just a joke!

Knock knock!

Who's there?

Abel!

Abel who?

Abel to see you if you open up!

Knock knock!

Who's there?

Conga!

Conga who?

Conga on standing outside all day!

Knock knock!

Who's there?

Colin!

Colin who?

I'm Colin Mom if you do not open the door!

Knock knock!

Who's there?

Oil!

Oil who?

Oil beat you up if you don't open the door!

Knock knock!

Who's there?

Cereal!

Cereal who?

Cereal pleasure to finally meet you!

Knock knock!

Who's there?

Albert!

Albert who!

Albert you don't know who this is!

Knock knock!

Who's there?

Aldo!

Aldo who?

Aldo anywhere with you!

Knock knock!

Who's there?

Costa!

Costa who?

Costa lot!

Knock knock!

Who's there?

Clare!

Clare who?

Clare your throat before you speak!

Knock knock!

Who's there?

A Fred!

A Fred who?

Who's a Fred of the Big Bad Wolf?

Knock knock!

Who's there?

Aitch!

Aitch who?

Bless You!

Knock knock!

Who's there?

Neil!

Neil who?

Neil down to your leader!

Knock knock!

Who's there?

Althea!

Althea who?

Althea when you open the door!

Knock knock!

Who's there?

May!

May who?

May I come in?

Knock knock!

Who's there?

Alf!

Alf who?

I pay Alf the rent here. Let me in!

Knock knock!

Who's there?

Ocelot!

Ocelot who?

You Ocelot of questions, don't you?

Knock knock!

Who's there?

Agatha!

Agatha who?

Agatha headache. Do you have an aspirin?

Knock knock!

Who's there?

Agent!

Agent who?

Agentle breeze!

Knock knock!

Who's there?

Keri!

Keri who?

Keri out the trash!

Knock knock!

Who's there?

Aladdin!

Aladdin who?

Aladdin the street wants a word with you!

Knock knock!

Who's there?

Alba!

Alba who?

Alba in the kitchen if you need me!

Knock knock!

Who's there?

Coffin!

Coffin who?

Coffin and spluttering!

Knock knock!

Who's there?

Coda!

Coda who?

Coda paint!

Knock knock!

Who's there?

Alec!

Alec who?

Alec-tricity. Isn't that a shock!

Knock knock!

Who's there?

Alma!

Alma who?

Alma money is gone. Can I borrow some?

Knock knock!

Who's there?

Jenny Linn!

Jenny Linn who?

Jenny Linn me some money please!

Knock knock!

Who's there?

Aileen!

Aileen who?

Aileen against the door until you open it!

Knock knock!

Who's there?

Noah!

Noah who?

Noah one will let me in!

Knock knock!

Who's there?

Alaska!

Alaska who?

Alaska my parents if I can go!

Knock knock!

Who's there?

Manny!

Manny who?

Manny times I have knocked on this door!

Knock knock!

Who's there?

Alligator!

Alligator who?

Alligator for his birthday was a card!

Knock knock!

Who's there?

Yucca!

Yucca who?

Yucca open the door and find out!

Knock knock!

Who's there?

Aleta!

Aleta who?

Aleta from the bill man!

Knock knock!

Who's there?

Alpaca!

Alpaca who?

Alpaca lunch for us to eat later!

Knock knock!

Who's there?

Jamaica!

Jamaica who?

Jamaica mistake if you don't open up!

Knock knock!

Who's there?

Alfred!

Alfred who!

Alfred of the dog! Open the door!

Knock knock!

Who's there?

Ina!

Ina who?

Ina get in this house sooner or later!

Knock knock!

Who's there?

Hugo!

Hugo who?

Hugo first!

Knock knock!

Who's there?

Caitlin!

Caitlin who?

Caitlin you my shoes. I'm wearing them today!

Knock knock!

Who's there?

Toby!

Toby who?

Toby or not to be? That is the question.

Knock knock!

Who's there?

Bosnia!

Bosnia who?

Bosnia bell on this door last time?

Knock knock!

Who's there?

Nunya!

Nunya who?

Nunya business!

Knock knock!

Who's there?

Juno!

Juno who?

Juno how long I've been knocking on this door?

Knock knock!

Who's there?

Yule!

Yule who?

Yule never guess!

Knock knock!

Who's there?

Icy!

Icy who?

Icy you! Let me in!

Knock knock!

Who's there?

Alex Plane!

Alex Plane who?

Alex Plane the details later!

Knock knock!

Who's there?

Bull!

Bull who?

Bull the door closed when you come in!

Knock knock!

Who's there?

Alka!

Alka who?

Alka pone!

Knock knock!

Who's there?

Alexander!

Alexander who?

Alexander friend are coming over soon!

Knock knock!

Who's there?

Tennessee!

Tennessee who?

You're the only Tennessee tonight!

Knock knock!

Who's there?

Texas!

Texas who?

Texas are rising every year!

Knock knock!

Who's there?

Alda!

Alda who?

Alda time you knew who it was!

Knock knock!

Who's there?

Beethoven!

Beethoven who?

Beethoven is too hot to touch!

Knock knock!

Who's there?

Abby!

Abby who?

Abby C D E F G!

Knock knock!

Who's there?

Buggy!

Buggy who?

This new app I downloaded is very buggy!

Knock knock!

Who's there?

Alexia!

Alexia who?

Alexia again to open this door right now!

Knock knock!

Who's there?

Bass!

Bass who?

Bass the salt please!

Knock knock!

Who's there?

Allison!

Allison who?

Allison to you if you will listen to me!

Knock knock!

Who's there?

Bobby!

Bobby who?

Bobby for apples at the birthday party!

Knock knock!

Who's there?

Mabel!

Mabel who?

You can have Mabel syrup on your pancakes!

Knock knock!

Who's there?

Olive!

Olive who?

Open up! Olive here too!

Knock knock!

Who's there?

Toucan!

Toucan who?

Toucan open up this door!

Knock knock!

Who's there?

Bassoon!

Bassoon who?

Bassoon things will get better!

Knock knock!

Who's there?

Al!

Al who?

Al lied!

Knock knock!

Who's there?

Leave.

Leave who?

LEAVE A REVIEW!

About the Author

Jimmy Giggles has always had a passion for making others laugh. As a child, he would use humor and comedy to bring a smile to the faces of friends and family.

Today he continues this with his jokes and comedy. Jimmy Giggles is known worldwide for his funny jokes, hilarious puns, and witty comedy.

You can find more of Jimmy's books on Amazon by searching:
JIMMY GIGGLES

Made in the USA
Middletown, DE
02 January 2017